Martinus Scriblerus's

Peri Bathous

or

The Art of Sinking in Poetry

Alexander Pope

ONEWORLD
CLASSICS

ONEWORLD CLASSICS LTD
London House
243-253 Lower Mortlake Road
Richmond
Surrey TW9 2LL
United Kingdom
www.oneworldclassics.com

The Art of Sinking in Poetry first published in 1727
This edition first published by Oneworld Classics Limited in 2009
Edited text and notes © Oneworld Classics Limited, 2009

Printed in Great Britain by CPI Antony Rowe

ISBN: 978-1-84749-105-3

All the pictures in this volume are reprinted with permission or presumed to be in the public domain. Every effort has been made to ascertain and acknowledge their copyright status, but should there have been any unwitting oversight on our part, we would be happy to rectify the error in subsequent printings.

All rights reserved. No part of this publication may be reproduced, stored in or introduced into a retrieval system, or transmitted, in any form or by any means (electronic, mechanical, photocopying, recording or otherwise), without the prior written permission of the publisher. This book is sold subject to the condition that it shall not be resold, lent, hired out or otherwise circulated without the express prior consent of the publisher.

Contents

The Art of Sinking in Poetry

1

I T HATH BEEN LONG – my dear countrymen* – the subject
of my concern and surprise that whereas numberless po-
ets, critics and orators have compiled and digested the art of
ancient poesy, there hath not arisen among us one person so
public-spirited as to perform the like for the modern. Al-
though it is universally known that our every-way industri-
ous moderns, both in the weight of their writings and in the
velocity of their judgements, do so infinitely excel the said
ancients.

Nevertheless, too true it is that while a plain and direct
road is paved to their ὕψος,* or "sublime", no track has
been yet chalked out to arrive at our βάθος, or "profound".
The Latins, as they came between the Greeks and us, make
use of the word *altitudo*, which implies equally height and
depth. Wherefore considering with no small grief how
many promising geniuses of this age are wandering – as I
may say – in the dark without a guide, I have undertaken
this arduous but necessary task to lead them as it were by the
hand and, step by step, the gentle downhill way to the *bathos*

3

– the bottom, the end, the central point, the *non plus ultra* of true modern poesy.

When I consider – my dear countrymen – the extent, fertility and populousness of our lowlands of Parnassus, the flourishing state of our trade and the plenty of our manufacture, there are two reflections which administer great occasion of surprise: the one, that all dignities and honours should be bestowed upon the exceeding few meagre inhabitants of the top of the mountain; the other, that our own nation should have arrived to that pitch of greatness it now possesses without any regular system of laws. As to the first, it is with great pleasure I have observed of late the gradual decay of delicacy and refinement among mankind, who are become too reasonable to require that we should labour with infinite pains to come up to the taste of those mountaineers, when they without any may condescend to ours. But as we have now an unquestionable majority on our side, I doubt not that we shall shortly be able to level the highlanders, and procure a further vent for our own product, which is already so much relished, encouraged and rewarded by the nobility and gentry of Great Britain.

Therefore, to supply our former defect, I propose to collect the scattered rules of our art into regular institutes, from the example and practice of the deep geniuses of our nation – imitating herein my predecessors, the master of Alexander and the secretary of the renowned Zenobia.* And in this my undertaking I am the more animated as I expect more success than has attended even those great critics, since their laws – though they might be good – have ever been slackly executed, and their precepts, however strict, obeyed only by fits, and by a very small number.

At the same time I intend to do justice upon our neighbours, inhabitants of the upper Parnassus, who taking advantage of the rising ground are perpetually throwing down rubbish, dirt and stones upon us, never suffering us to live in peace. These men, while they enjoy the crystal stream of Helicon, envy us our common water, which – thank our stars – though it is somewhat muddy, flows in much greater abundance. Nor is this the greatest injustice we have to complain of, for though it is evident that we never made the least attempt or inroad into their territories, but lived contented in our native fens, they have often not only committed petty larcenies on our borders, but driven the country and carried off at once whole cartloads of our manufacture; to reclaim some of which stolen goods is part of the design of this treatise.

For we shall see in the course of this work that our greatest adversaries have sometimes descended towards us, and doubtless might now and then have arrived at the *bathos* itself, had it not been for that mistaken opinion they all entertained that the rules of the ancients were equally necessary to the moderns – than which there cannot be a more grievous error, as will be amply proved in the following discourse.

And indeed when any of these have gone so far as by the light of their own genius to attempt upon new models, it is wonderful to observe how nearly they have approached us in those particular pieces, though in all their others they differed *toto cœlo** from us.

2

That the bathos*, or profound, is the natural taste of man and, in particular, of the present age.*

T HE TASTE OF THE BATHOS is implanted by nature itself in the soul of man, till perverted by custom or example he is taught, or rather compelled, to relish the sublime. Accordingly we see the unprejudiced minds of children delight only in such productions and in such images as our true modern writers set before them. I have observed how fast the general taste is returning to this first simplicity and innocence, and if the intent of all poetry be to divert and instruct, certainly that kind which diverts and instructs the greatest number is to be preferred. Let us look round among the admirers of poetry: we shall find those who have a taste of the sublime to be very few, but the profound strikes universally and is adapted to every capacity. 'Tis a fruitless undertaking to write for men of a nice and foppish gusto – whom, after all, it is almost impossible to please – and it is still more chimerical to write for posterity, of whose taste we cannot make any judgement and

7

whose applause we can never enjoy. It must be confessed: our wiser authors have a present end:

Et prodesse volunt, et delectare Poetæ.*

Their true design is profit or gain, in order to acquire which 'tis necessary to procure applause by administering pleasure to the reader. From whence it follows demonstrably that their productions must be suited to the present taste, and I cannot but congratulate our age on this peculiar felicity: that though we have made indeed great progress in all other branches of luxury, we are not yet debauched with any high relish in poetry, but are in this one taste less nice than our ancestors. If an art is to be estimated by its success, I appeal to experience whether there have not been, in proportion to their number, as many starving good poets as bad ones?

Nevertheless, in making gain the principal end of our art, far be it from me to exclude any great geniuses of rank or fortune from diverting themselves this way. They ought to be praised no less than those princes who pass their vacant hours in some ingenious mechanical or manual art, and to such as these it would be ingratitude not to own that our art has been often infinitely indebted.

3

The necessity of the bathos, *physically considered.*

Furthermore, it were great cruelty and injustice if all such authors as cannot write in the other way were prohibited from writing at all. Against this I draw an argument from what seems to me an undoubted physical maxim: that poetry is a natural or morbid secretion from the brain. As I would not suddenly stop a cold in the head, or dry up my neighbour's issue, I would as little hinder him from necessary writing. It may be affirmed with great truth that there is hardly any human creature past childhood but at one time or other has had some poetical evacuation, and no question was much the better for it in his health – so true is the saying: "*Nascimur poetæ*".* Therefore is the desire of writing properly termed *pruritus* – the titillation of the generative faculty of the brain – and the person is said to "conceive". Now, such as conceive must bring forth. I have known a man thoughtful, melancholy and raving for divers days, but forthwith grow wonderfully easy, lightsome and cheerful upon a discharge of the peccant humour in exceeding purulent metre. Nor can I question but an abundance of untimely deaths are occasioned by want of this laudable vent of unruly passions – yea, perhaps in poor wretches, which is very lamentable – for mere want of pen, ink and paper. From hence it follows that a suppression of the very worst poetry is of dangerous consequence to the State. We find by experience that the same humours which vent themselves in summer in ballads and sonnets are condensed by the winter's cold into pamphlets and speeches for and against the ministry. Nay, I know not but many times a piece of poetry may be the most innocent composition of a minister himself.

It is therefore manifest that mediocrity ought to be allowed, yea, indulged, to the good subjects of England. Nor can I conceive how the world has swallowed the contrary as a maxim upon the single authority of that Horace.* Why should the golden mean and quintessence of all virtues be deemed so offensive only in this art? Or coolness or mediocrity be so amiable a quality in a man and so detestable in a poet?

However, far be it from me to compare these writers with those great spirits who are born with a *vivacité de pesanteur* – or, as an English author calls it, an "alacrity of sinking"* – and who, by strength of nature alone, can excel. All I mean is to evince the necessity of rules to these lesser geniuses, as well as the usefulness of them to the greater.

4

That there is an art of the bathos, *or profound.*

WE COME NOW TO PROVE that there is an art of sinking in poetry. Is there not an architecture of vaults and cellars as well as of lofty domes and pyramids? Is there not as much skill and labour in making of dykes as in raising of mounts? Is there not an art of diving as well as of flying? And will any sober practitioner affirm that a diving engine is not of singular use in making him long-winded, assisting his sight and furnishing him with other ingenious means of keeping underwater?

If we search the authors of antiquity, we shall find as few to have been distinguished in the true profound as in the true sublime. And the very same thing – as it appears from Longinus – had been imagined of that, as now of this: namely that it was entirely the gift of nature. I grant that to excel in the *bathos* a genius is requisite, yet the rules of art must be allowed so far useful as to add weight or, as I may say, hang on lead, to facilitate and enforce our descent, to guide us to the most advantageous declivities and habituate our imagination to a depth of thinking. Many there are that can fall, but few can arrive at the felicity of falling gracefully. Much more, for a man who is amongst the lowest of the creation at the very bottom of the atmosphere, to descend beneath himself is not so easy a task unless he calls in art to his assistance. It is with the *bathos* as with small beer, which is indeed vapid and insipid if left at large and let abroad, but being by our rules confined and well stopped, nothing grows so frothy, pert and bouncing.

The sublime of nature is the sky, the sun, moon, stars, etc. The profound of nature is gold, pearls, precious stones and the treasures of the deep, which are inestimable as unknown. But all that lies between these, as corn, flowers, fruits, animals and things for the mere use of man are of mean price, and so common as not to be greatly esteemed by the curious, it being certain that anything of which we know the true use cannot be invaluable – which affords a solution why common sense hath either been totally despised or held in small repute by the greatest modern critics and authors.

5

Of the true genius for the profound,
and by what it is constituted.

A ND I WILL VENTURE to lay it down as the first maxim
and cornerstone of this our art that whoever would
excel therein must studiously avoid, detest and turn his head
from all the ideas, ways and workings of that pestilent foe
to wit and destroyer of fine figures, which is known by the
name of common sense. His business must be to contract the
true *goût de travers** and to acquire a most happy, uncommon,
unaccountable way of thinking.

He is to consider himself as a grotesque painter whose works
would be spoilt by an imitation of nature or uniformity of
design. He is to mingle bits of the most various or discordant
kinds – landscape, history, portraits, animals – and connect
them with a great deal of flourishing, by heads or tails, as it
shall please his imagination, and contribute to his principal
end, which is to glare by strong oppositions of colours and
surprise by contrariety of images.

Serpentes avibus geminentur, tigribus agni.*

His design ought to be like a labyrinth, out of which nobody can get you clear but himself. And since the great art of all poetry is to mix truth and fiction, in order to join the credible with the surprising our author shall produce the credible by painting nature in her lowest simplicity, and the surprising by contradicting common opinion. In the very manners he will affect the marvellous: he will draw Achilles with the patience of Job, a prince talking like a jack pudding, a maid of honour selling bargains, a footman speaking like a philosopher and a fine gentleman like a scholar. Whoever is conversant in modern plays may make a most noble collection of this kind and, at the same time, form a complete body of modern ethics and morality.

Nothing seemed more plain to our great authors than that the world had long been weary of natural things. How much the contrary is formed to please is evident from the universal applause daily given to the admirable entertainments of harlequins and magicians on our stage.* When an audience behold a coach turned into a wheelbarrow, a conjuror into an old woman, or a man's head where his heels should be, how are they struck with transport and delight! Which can only be imputed to this cause: that each object is changed into that which hath been suggested to them by their own low ideas before.

He ought therefore to render himself master of this happy and antinatural way of thinking to such a degree as to be able, on the appearance of any object, to furnish his imagination with ideas infinitely below it. And his eyes should be like unto the wrong end of a perspective glass, by which all the objects of nature are lessened.

For example, when a true genius looks upon the sky, he immediately catches the idea of a piece of blue lutestring or a child's mantle.

> The skies, whose spreading volumes scarce have room,
> Spun thin, and wove in Nature's finest loom,
> The newborn world in their soft lap embraced,
> And all around their starry mantle cast.

If he looks upon a tempest, he shall have the image of a tumbled bed, and describe a succeeding calm in this manner:

> The ocean joyed to see the tempest fled,
> New lays his waves and smoothes his ruffled bed.

The triumphs and acclamations of the angels at the creation of the universe present to his imagination the rejoicings of the Lord Mayor's Day, and he beholds those glorious beings celebrating the creator by huzzahing, making illuminations and flinging squibs, crackers and sky rockets.

Glorious illuminations, made on high
By all the stars and planets of the sky,
In just degrees and shining order placed,
Spectators charmed, and the blessed dwelling graced.
Thro' all th'enlightened air swift fireworks flew,
Which with repeated shouts glad cherubs threw,
Comets ascended with their sweeping train,
Then fell in starry showers and glittering rain.
In air ten thousand meteors blazing hung,
Which from th'eternal battlements were flung.*

If a man who is violently fond of wit will sacrifice to that passion his friend or his God, would it not be a shame if he who is smit with the love of the *bathos* should not sacrifice to it all other transitory regards? You shall hear a zealous Protestant deacon invoke a saint, and modestly beseech her only to change the course of providence and destiny for the sake of three or four weighty lines:

Look down, blessed saint, with pity then look down,
Shed on this land thy kinder influence,
And guide us through the mists of providence,
In which we stray...*

Neither will he, if a goodly simile come in his way, scruple to affirm himself an eyewitness of things never yet beheld by man, or never in existence, as thus:

Thus have I seen, in Araby the blessed,
A Phoenix couched upon her fun'ral nest.*

But to convince you that nothing is so great which a marvellous genius, prompted by this laudable zeal, is not able to lessen, hear how the most sublime of all beings is represented in the following images.

First he is a painter:

Sometimes the Lord of Nature in the air
Spreads forth his clouds, his sable canvas, where
His pencil, dipped in heavenly colour bright
Paints his fair rainbow, charming to the sight.

Now he is a chemist:

Th'almighty chemist does his work prepare,
Pours down his waters on the thirsty plain,
Digests his lightning, and distils his rain.

Now he is a wrestler:

> Me in his griping arms th'eternal took,
> And with such mighty force my body shook
> That the strong grasp my members sorely bruised,
> Broke all my bones, and all my sinews loosed.

Now a recruiting officer:

> For clouds the sunbeams levy fresh supplies,
> And raise recruits of vapours – which arise,
> Drawn from the seas, to muster in the skies.

Now a peaceable guarantee:

> In leagues of peace the neighbours did agree
> And, to maintain them, God was guarantee.

Then he is an attorney:

> Job, as a vile offender, God indites,
> And terrible decrees against me writes.
> God will not be my advocate,
> My cause to manage or debate.

In the following lines he is a gold-beater:

Who the rich metal beats and then, with care,
Unfolds the golden leaves to gild the fields of air.

Then a fuller:

> ...th'exhaling reeks that secret rise,
> Born on rebounding sunbeams thro' the skies,
> Are thickened, wrought and whitened till they grow
> A heavenly fleece...

A mercer, or packer:

> Didst thou one end of air's wide curtain hold,
> And help the bales of aether to unfold?
> Say, which cerulean pile was by thy hand unrolled?

A butler:

> He measures all the drops with wondrous skill,
> Which the black clouds, his floating bottles, fill.

And a baker:

> God in the wilderness his table spread,
> And in his airy ovens baked their bread.*

6

Of the several kinds of geniuses in the profound,
and the marks and characters of each.

I DOUBT NOT BUT THE READER, by this cloud of examples, begins to be convinced of the truth of our assertion that the *bathos* is an art, and that the genius of no mortal whatever, following the mere ideas of nature and unassisted with a habitual – nay, laborious – peculiarity of thinking, could arrive at images so wonderfully low and unaccountable. The great author from whose treasury we have drawn all these instances – the father of the *bathos* and indeed the Homer of it – has like that immortal Greek confined his labours to the greater poetry, and thereby left room for others to acquire a due share of praise in inferior kinds. Many painters who could never hit a nose or an eye have with felicity copied a smallpox, or been admirable at a toad or a red herring. And seldom are we without geniuses for still life, which they can work up and stiffen with incredible accuracy.

A universal genius rises not in an age – but when he rises, armies rise in him! He pours forth five or six epic poems with greater facility than five or six pages can be produced by an elaborate and servile copier after nature or the ancients. It is affirmed by Quintilian that the same genius which made Germanicus so great a general would with equal application have made him an excellent heroic poet. In like manner, reasoning from the affinity there appears between arts and sciences, I doubt not but an active catcher of butterflies, a careful and fanciful pattern-drawer, an industrious collector of shells, a laborious and tuneful bagpiper or a diligent breeder of tame rabbits might severally excel in their respective parts of the *bathos*.

I shall range these confined and less copious geniuses under proper classes and – the better to give their pictures to the reader – under the names of animals of some sort or other; whereby he will be enabled, at the first sight of such as shall daily come forth, to know to what kind to refer, and with what authors to compare them.*

1. The flying fishes – these are writers who now and then rise upon their fins and fly out of the profound, but their wings are soon dry and they drop down to the bottom. G.S., A.H., C.G.*

2. The swallows are authors that are eternally skimming and fluttering up and down, but all their agility is employed to catch flies. L.T., W.P., Lord R.*

CHAPTER 6

3. The ostriches are such whose heaviness rarely permits them to raise themselves from the ground. Their wings are of no use to lift them up, and their motion is between flying and walking, but then they run very fast. D.F., L.E., the Hon. E.H.*

4. The parrots are they that repeat another's words, in such a hoarse, odd voice that makes them seem their own. W.B., W.H., C.C., the Reverend D.D.*

5. The didappers are authors that keep themselves long out of sight, underwater, and come up now and then where you least expected them. L.W. — D. Esq., the Hon. Sir W.Y.*

6. The porpoises are unwieldy and big. They put all their numbers into a great turmoil and tempest, but whenever they appear in plain light – which is seldom – they are only shapeless and ugly monsters. J.D., C.G., J.O.*

7. The frogs are such as can neither walk nor fly, but can leap and bound to admiration. They live generally in the bottom of a ditch, and make a great noise whenever they thrust their heads above water. E.W., J.M. Esq., T.D. Gent.*

8. The eels are obscure authors that wrap themselves up in their own mud, but are mighty nimble and pert. L.W., L.T., P.M., General C.*

9. The tortoises are slow and chill and, like pastoral writers, delight much in gardens. They have for the most part a fine embroidered shell and, underneath it, a heavy lump. A.P., W.B., L.E., the Rt. Hon. E. of S.*

These are the chief characteristics of the *bathos*, and in each of these kinds we have the comfort to be blessed with sundry and manifold choice spirits in this our island.

7

Of the profound, when it consists in the thought.

W E HAVE ALREADY LAID DOWN THE PRINCIPLES upon which our author is to proceed, and the manner of forming his thoughts by familiarizing his mind to the lowest objects – to which it may be added that vulgar conversation will greatly contribute. There is no question but the garret or the printer's boy may often be discerned in the compositions made in such scenes and company, and much of Mr Curll* himself has been insensibly infused into the works of his learned writers.

The physician, by the study and inspection of urine and ordure, approves himself in the science, and in like sort should our author accustom and exercise his imagination upon the dregs of nature.

This will render his thoughts truly and fundamentally low, and carry him many fathoms beyond mediocrity. For certain it is – though some lukewarm heads imagine they may be safe by temporizing between the extremes – that where there is a triticalness* or mediocrity in the thought, it can never be sunk into the genuine and perfect *bathos* by the most elaborate low expression. It can, at most, be only carefully obscured, or metaphorically debased. But 'tis the thought alone that strikes and gives the whole that spirit which we admire and stare at. For instance, in that ingenious piece on a lady's drinking in the bath waters:

> She drinks! She drinks! Behold the matchless Dame!
> To her 'tis water, but to us 'tis flame:
> Thus fire is water, water fire, by turns,
> And the same stream at once both cools and burns.

What can be more easy and unaffected than the diction of these verses? 'Tis the turn of thought alone, and the variety of imagination that charm and surprise us. And when the same lady goes into the bath, the thought – as in justness it ought – goes still deeper.

> Venus beheld her, 'midst her crowd of slaves,
> And thought herself just risen from the waves.

How much out of the way of common sense is this reflection of Venus, not knowing herself from the lady?

CHAPTER 7

Of the same nature is that noble mistake of a frighted stag in full chase, of which the poet:

> Hears his own feet, and thinks they sound like more;
> And fears the hind feet will o'ertake the fore.*

So astonishing as these are, they yield to the following, which is profundity itself:

> None but himself can be his parallel.*

Unless it may seem borrowed from that master of a show in Smithfield who writ in large letters, over the picture of his elephant: "This is the greatest elephant in the world, except himself."

However, our next instance is certainly an original. Speaking of a beautiful infant:

> So fair thou art that if great Cupid be
> A child, as poets say, sure thou art he.
> Fair Venus would mistake thee for her own,
> Did not thy eyes proclaim thee not her son.
> There all the lightnings of thy mother's shine,
> And with a fatal brightness kill in thine.

First he is Cupid, then he is not Cupid; first Venus would mistake him, then she would not mistake him; next his eyes are his mother's; and lastly they are not his mother's, but his own.

Another author, describing a poet that shines forth amidst a circle of critics:

> Thus Phoebus thro' the zodiac takes his way,
> And amid monsters rises into day.*

What a peculiarity is here of invention! The author's pencil, like the wand of Circe, turns all into monsters at a stroke. A great genius takes things in the lump without stopping at minute considerations. In vain might the ram, the bull, the goat, the lion, the crab, the scorpion, the fishes all stand in his way as mere natural animals. Much more it might be pleaded that a pair of scales, an old man and two innocent children were no monsters – there were only the centaur and the maid that could be esteemed out of nature. But what of that? With a boldness peculiar to these daring geniuses, what he found not monsters, he made so.

8

Of the profound consisting in the circumstances,
and of amplification and periphrase in general.

W HAT IN A GREAT MEASURE distinguishes other writers
from ours is their choosing and separating such cir-
cumstances in a description as illustrate or elevate the sub-
ject.

The circumstances which are most natural are obvious,
therefore not astonishing or peculiar. But those that are far-
fetched or unexpected or hardly compatible will surprise
prodigiously. These therefore we must principally hunt
out; but, above all, preserve a laudable prolixity, presenting
the whole and every side at once of the image to view. For
choice and distinction are not only a curb to the spirit and
limit the descriptive faculty, but also lessen the book, which is
frequently of the worst consequence of all to our author.

When Job says in short, "He washed his feet in butter" – a
circumstance some poets would have softened or passed over
– hear how it is spread out by the great genius:

With teats distended with their milky store,
Such num'rous lowing herds, before my door,
Their painful burden to unload did meet,
That we with butter might have washed our feet.

How cautious and particular! He had – says our author – so many herds... which herds thrived so well, and thriving so well gave so much milk, and that milk produced so much butter that, if he *did not*, he *might* have washed his feet in it.

The ensuing description of hell is no less remarkable in the circumstances:

In flaming heaps the raging ocean rolls,
Whole livid waves involve despairing souls;
The liquid burnings dreadful colours show –
Some deeply red, and others faintly blue.*

Could the most minute Dutch painter have been more exact? How inimitably circumstantial is this also of a warhorse:

His eyeballs burn, he wounds the smoking plain,
And knots of scarlet ribbon deck his mane.*

Of certain cudgel players:

> They brandish high in air their threat'ning staves,
> Their hands a woven guard of osier saves,
> In which they fix their hazel weapon's end.

Who would not think the poet had passed his whole life at wakes in such laudable diversions? He even teaches us how to hold and to make a cudgel!

Periphrase is another great aid to prolixity, being a diffused circumlocutory manner of expressing a known idea which should be so mysteriously couched as to give the reader the pleasure of guessing what it is that the author can possibly mean – and a surprise when he finds it.

The poet I last mentioned is incomparable in this figure:

> A waving sea of heads was round me spread,
> And still fresh streams the gazing deluge fed.*

Here is a waving sea of heads, which by a fresh stream of heads grows to be a gazing deluge of heads. You come at last to find it means "a great crowd".

How pretty and how genteel is the following:

> Nature's confectioner...
> Whose suckets are moist alchemy
> The still of his refining mould,
> Minting the garden into gold.*

What is this but a bee gathering honey?

> Little siren of the stage,
> Empty warbler, breathing lyre,
> Wanton gale of fond desire,
> Tuneful mischief, vocal spell...*

Who would think this was only a poor gentlewoman that sung finely?

We may define amplification to be making the most of a thought – it is the spinning wheel of the *bathos* that draws out and spreads it in the finest thread. There are amplifiers who can extend half a dozen thin thoughts over a whole folio, but for which the tale of many a vast romance and the substance of many a fair volume might be reduced into the size of a primer.

In the Book of Job are these words: "Hast thou commanded the morning, and caused the day spring to know his place?" How is this extended by the most celebrated amplifier of our age?

> Canst thou set forth th'ethereal mines on high,
> Which the refulgent ore of light supply?
> Is the celestial furnace to thee known
> In which I melt the golden metal down?

Treasures from whence I deal out light as fast
As all my stars and lavish suns can waste.

The same author hath amplified a passage in the 104th Psalm: "He looks on the earth, and it trembles. He touches the hills, and they smoke."

The hills forget they're fixed, and in their fright
Cast off their weight and ease themselves for flight:
The woods, with terror winged, outfly the wind,
And leave the heavy, panting hills behind.*

You here see the hills not only trembling, but shaking off their woods from their backs to run the faster. After this, you are presented with a foot race of mountains and woods, where the woods distance the mountains, that like corpulent pursy fellows come puffing and panting a vast way behind them.

9

Of imitation and the manner of imitating.

THAT THE TRUE AUTHORS OF THE PROFOUND are to imitate diligently the examples in their own way is not to be questioned, and that divers have by this means attained to a depth whereunto their own weight could not have carried them is evident by sundry instances. Who sees not that De F*** was not the poetical son of Withers, T***te of Ogilby, E. W***rd of John Taylor and E***n of Bl***k***re?* Therefore, when we sit down to write, let us bring some great author to our mind and ask ourselves this question: "How would Sir Richard have said this? Do I express myself as simply as A. Ph***, or flow my numbers with the quiet thoughtlessness of Mr W***st***d?"*

But it may seem somewhat strange to assert that our proficient should also read the works of those poets who have excelled in the sublime – yet this is not a paradox. As Virgil is said to have read Ennius out of his dunghill to draw gold, so may our author read Shakespeare, Milton and

Dryden for the contrary end: to bury their gold in his own dunghill. A true genius, when he finds anything lofty or shining in them, will have the skill to bring it down, take off the gloss, or quite discharge the colour by some ingenious circumstance or periphrase, some addition or diminution, or by some of those figures the use of which we shall show in our next chapter.

The book of Job is acknowledged to be infinitely sublime, and yet has not our father of the *bathos* reduced it in every page? Is there a passage in all Virgil more painted up and laboured than the description of Etna in the third *Aeneid*?

> ...*Horrificis juxta tonat Aetna ruinis,*
> *Interdumque atram prorumpit ad aethera nubem,*
> *Turbine fumantem piceo, et candente favilla,*
> *Attollitque globos flammarum, et sidera lambit.*
> *Interdum scopulos avulsaque viscera montis*
> *Erigit eructans, liquefactaque saxa sub auras*
> *Cum gemitu glomerat, fundoque exaestuat imo.**

(I beg pardon of the gentle English reader, and such of our writers as understand not Latin.) But lo! How this is taken down by our British poet, by this single happy thought of throwing the mountain into a fit of the colic!

Etna, and all the burning mountains, find
Their kindled stores with inbred stores of wind
Blown up to rage and, roaring out, complain
As torn with inward gripes and torturing pain:
Lab'ring, they cast their dreadful vomit round,
And with their melted bowels, spread the ground.*

Horace, in search of the sublime, struck his head against the stars,* but Empedocles, to fathom the profound, threw himself into Etna.* And who but would imagine our excellent modern had also been there, from this description?

Imitation is of two sorts: the first is when we force to our own purposes the thoughts of others; the second consists in copying the imperfections or blemishes of celebrated authors. I have seen a play professedly writ in the style of Shakespeare wherein the greatest resemblance lay in one single line:

And so good morrow t'ye, good Master Lieutenant.*

And sundry poems in imitation of Milton where, with the utmost exactness, and not so much as one exception, nevertheless was constantly "nathless", embroidered was constantly "broidered", hermits were "eremites", disdained was "sdeigned", shady "umbrageous", enterprise "emprize", pagan "paynim", pinions "pennons", sweet "dulcet", orchards "orchats", bridgework "pontifical" – nay, her was "hir", and their was "thir" through the whole poem. And in very deed, there is no other way by which the true modern poet could read to any purpose the works of such men as Milton and Shakespeare.

It may be expected that, like other critics, I should next speak of the passions. But as the main end and principal effect of the *bathos* is to produce tranquillity of mind – and sure it is a better design to promote sleep than madness – we have little to say on this subject. Nor will the short bounds of this discourse allow us to treat at large of the emollients and opiates of poesy, of the cool and the manner of producing it, or of the methods used by our authors in managing the passions. I shall but transiently remark that nothing contributes so much to the cool as the use of wit in expressing passion. The true genius rarely fails of points, conceits and proper similes on such occasions. This we may term the "pathetic epigrammatical", in which even puns are made use of with good success. Hereby our best authors have avoided throwing themselves or their readers into any indecent transports.

But forasmuch as it is sometimes needful to excite the passions of our antagonist in the polemic way, the true students in the low have constantly taken their methods from low life, where they observed that, to move anger, use is made of scolding and railing – to move love, of bawdry – to beget favour and friendship, of gross flattery – and to produce fear, by calumniating an adversary with crimes obnoxious to the State. As for shame, it is a silly passion of which, as our authors are incapable themselves, so they would not produce it in others.

10

Of tropes and figures, and first of the
variegating, confusing and reversing figures.

B UT WE PROCEED TO THE FIGURES. We cannot too earnestly recommend to our authors the study of the abuse of speech. They ought to lay it down as a principle to say nothing in the usual way but, if possible, in the direct contrary. Therefore the figures must be so turned as to manifest that intricate and wonderful cast of head which distinguishes all writers of this genius – or, as I may say, to refer exactly the mould in which they were formed, in all its inequalities, cavities, obliquities, odd crannies and distortions.

It would be endless – nay, impossible – to enumerate all such figures, but we shall content ourselves to range the principal which most powerfully contribute to the *bathos*, under three classes:

1. The variegating, confusing or reversing tropes and figures.

2.   The magnifying

and

3.   The diminishing.

We cannot avoid giving to these the Greek or Roman names, but in tenderness to our countrymen and fellow writers – many of whom, however exquisite, are wholly ignorant of those languages – we have also explained them in our mother tongue.

   Of the first sort, nothing so much conduces to the abuse of speech as the

Catachresis

A master of this will say:

> Mow the beard,
> Shave the grass,
> Pin the plank,
> Nail my sleeve.

From whence results the same kind of pleasure to the mind as doth to the eye when we behold Harlequin trimming himself with a hatchet, hewing down a tree with a razor, making his tea in a cauldron, and brewing his ale in a tea pot, to the incredible satisfaction of the British spectator. Another source of *bathos* is

The Metonymy

The inversion of causes for effects, of inventors for inventions etc.

> Laced in her cosins, new appeared the bride,
> A bubble boy and tompion at her side,
> And with an air divine her colmar plied,
> And "Oh!" she cries, "what slaves I round me see?
> Here a bright redcoat, there a smart toupee."*

The Synecdoche

Which consists in the use of a part for the whole – you may call a young woman sometimes "pretty face" and "pigs' eyes", and sometimes "snotty nose" and "draggle tail". Or of accidents for persons – as a lawyer is called "split cause", a tailor "prick louse", etc. Or of things belonging to a man, for the man himself – as a swordman, a gownman, a T***m-T***dman, a whitestaff,* a turnkey, etc.

The Aposiopesis

An excellent figure for the ignorant as "What shall I say?" when one has nothing to say, or "I can no more" when one really can no more – expressions which the gentle reader is so good as to never take in earnest.

The Metaphor

The first rule is to draw it from the lowest things, which is a certain way to sink the highest. As when you speak of the thunder of heaven say:

> The lords above are angry and talk big.*

If you would describe a rich man refunding his treasures, express it thus:

> Tho' he – as said – may riches gorge, the spoil
> Painful in massy vomit shall recoil.
> Soon shall he perish with a swift decay,
> Like his own ordure, cast with scorn away.

The second, that whenever you start a metaphor, you must be sure to run it down and pursue it as far as it can go. If you get the scent of a state negotiation, follow it in this manner:

The stones and all the elements with thee
Shall ratify a strict confederacy;
Wild beasts their savage temper shall forget,
And for a firm alliance with thee treat;
The finny tyrant of the spacious seas
Shall send a scaly embassy for peace:
His plighted faith the crocodile shall keep
And, seeing thee, for joy sincerely weep.

Or, if you represent the Creator denouncing war against the wicked, be sure not to omit one circumstance usual in proclaiming and levying war:

Envoys and agents, who by my command
Reside in Palestina's land,
To whom commissions I have given
To manage there the interests of Heaven –
Ye holy heralds who proclaim
Or war or peace, in mine your Master's name –
Ye pioneers of Heaven, prepare a road,
Make it plain, direct and broad…
For I in person will my people head;
　　…For the Divine Deliverer
Will on his march in majesty appear,
And needs the aid of no confederate pow'r.

Under the article of the confusing, we rank:

The Mixture of Figures

Which raises so many images as to give you no image at all. But its principal beauty is when it gives an idea just opposite to what it seemed meant to describe. Thus an ingenious artist, painting the spring, talks of a snow of blossoms, and thereby raises an unexpected picture of winter. Of this sort is the following:

> The gaping clouds pour lakes of sulphur down,
> Whole livid flashes sick'ning sunbeams drown.

What a noble confusion! Clouds, lakes, brimstone, flames, sunbeams, gaping, pouring, sickening, drowning all in two lines!

The Jargon

> Thy head shall rise, tho' buried in the dust,
> And 'midst the clouds his glittering turrets thrust.

Quære, what are the glittering turrets of a man's head?

Upon the shore, as frequent as the sand,
To meet the Prince, the glad Dimetians stand.

Quære, where these Dimetians stood and of what size they were?

Destruction's empire shall no longer last,
And desolation lie for ever waste.*

But for variegation and confusion of objects, nothing is more useful than

The Antithesis, or Seesaw

Whereby contraries and oppositions are balanced in such a way as to cause a reader to remain suspended between them, to his exceeding delight and recreation. Such are these on a lady who made herself appear out of size by hiding a young princess under her clothes:

While the kind nymph, changing her faultless shape,
Becomes unhandsome, handsomely to 'scape.*

On the maids of honour in mourning:

Sadly they charm, and dismally they please.*

       ...His eyes so bright
Let in the object, and let out the light.*

The gods look pale to see us look so red.*

       ...The fairies and their queen
In mantles blue came tripping o'er the green.*

All nature felt a reverential shock:
The sea stood still to see the mountains rock.*

11

The figures continued: of the
magnifying and diminishing figures.

A GENUINE WRITER OF THE PROFOUND will take care never to magnify any object without clouding it at the same time. His thought will appear in a true mist, and very unlike what it is in nature. It must always be remembered that darkness is an essential quality of the profound or, if there chance to be a glimmering, it must be as Milton expresses it:

No light, but rather darkness visible.

The chief figure of this sort is

The Hyperbole, or Impossible

For instance, of a lion:

He roared so loud, and looked so wondrous grim,
His very shadow durst not follow him.

Of a lady at dinner:

The silver whiteness that adorns thy neck
Sullies the plate, and makes the napkin black.*

Of the same:

…Th'obscureness of her birth
Cannot eclipse the lustre of her eyes,
Which make her all one light.*

Of a bull-baiting:

Up to the stars the sprawling mastiffs fly,
And add new monsters to the frighted sky.*

Of a scene of misery:

Behold a scene of misery and woe!
Here Argus soon might weep himself quite blind,
Even tho' he had Briareus' hundred hands
To wipe those hundred eyes…

And that modest request of two absent lovers:

> Ye gods! Annihilate but space and time,
> And make two lovers happy…

The Periphrasis

Which the moderns call the *circumbendibus*, whereof we have given examples in the ninth chapter, and shall again in the twelfth.

To the same class of the magnifying may be referred the following, which are so excellently modern that we have yet no name for them. In describing a country prospect:

> I'd call them mountains, but can't call them so,
> For fear to wrong them with a name too low;
> While the fair vales beneath so humbly lie
> That even humble seems a term too high.*

3. The third class remains of the diminishing figures – and first the anticlimax, where the second line drops quite short of the first, than which nothing creates greater surprise.

On the extent of the British arms:

Under the tropics is our language spoke,
And part of Flanders hath received our yoke.*

On a warrior:

And thou, Dalhousie, the great god of war,
Lieutenant Colonel to the Earl of Mar.*

On the valour of the English:

Nor death nor hell itself can keep them out,
　　…Nor fortified redoubt.*

At other times this figure operates in a larger extent, and when the gentle reader is in expectation of some great image, he either finds it surprisingly imperfect or is presented with something very low or quite ridiculous. A surprise resembling that of a curious person in a cabinet of antique statues who beholds on the pedestal the names of Homer or Cato but, looking up, finds Homer without a head, and nothing to be seen of Cato but his privy member. Such are these lines on a leviathan at sea:

His motion works and beats the oozy mud,
And with its slime incorporates the flood,

Till all th'encumbered, thick fermenting stream
Does one vast pot of boiling ointment seem.
Where'er he swims, he leaves along the lake
Such frothy furrows, such a foamy track,
That all the waters of the deep appear
Hoary with age, or grey with sudden fear.

But perhaps even these are excelled by the ensuing:

Now the resisted flames and fiery store,
By winds assaulted, in wide forges roar,
And raging seas flow down of melted ore.
Sometimes they hear long iron bars removed,
And to and fro huge heaps of cinders shoved.

The Vulgar

is also a species of the diminishing. By this, a spear flying
in the air is compared to a boy whistling as he goes on an
errand:

The mighty Stuffa threw a massy spear
Which, with its errand pleased, sung thro' the air.

A man raging with grief to a mastiff dog:

I cannot stifle this gigantic woe,
Nor on my raging grief a muzzle throw.

And clouds big with water to a woman in great necessity:

Distended with the waters in 'em pent,
The clouds hang deep in air, but hang unrent.*

The Infantine

This is when a poet grows so very simple as to think and talk
like a child. I shall take my examples from the greatest master
in this way. Hear how he fondles, like a mere stammerer:

Little charm of placid mien,
Miniature of beauty's queen,
Hither British muse of mine,
Hither, all ye Grecian nine,
With the lovely Graces three,
And your pretty nurseling see.

When the meadows next are seen,
Sweet enamel, white and green,
When again the lambkins play,
Pretty sportlings full of May,

Then the neck so white and round
(Little neck with brilliants bound)
And thy gentleness of mind
(Gentle from a gentle kind) etc.
Happy thrice, and thrice again,
Happiest he of happy men, etc.*

With the rest of those excellent lullabies of his composition.

How prettily he asks the sheep to teach him to bleat?

Teach me to grieve with bleating moan, my sheep.

Hear how a babe would reason on his nurse's death:

That ever she could die! – Oh most unkind!
To die and leave poor Colinet behind?
And yet – why blame I her?...

His shepherd reasons as much like an innocent, in love:

I love in secret all a beauteous maid,
And have my love in secret all repaid:
This coming night she does reserve for me.

The love of this maiden to him appears by her allowing him the reserve of one night from her other lovers, which you see he takes extremely kindly.

With no less simplicity does he suppose that shepherdesses tear their hair and beat their breasts at their own deaths:

> Ye brighter maids, faint emblems of my fair,
> With looks cast down, and with dishevelled hair,
> In bitter anguish beat your breasts and moan
> Her death untimely as it were your own.

The Inanity, or Nothingness

Of this the same author furnishes us with the most beautiful instances:

> Ah silly I, more silly than my sheep
> (Which on the flowery plain I once did keep).

> To the grave senate she could counsel give
> (Which with astonishment they did receive).

> He whom loud cannon could not terrify,
> Falls (from the grandeur of his majesty)*

The noise returning with returning light,

What did it?

Dispersed the silence, and dispelled the night.*

The glories of proud London to survey,
The sun himself shall rise – by break of day.*

The Expletive

Admirably exemplified in the epithets of many authors:

Th'umbrageous shadow and the verdant green,
The running current and odorous fragrance,
Cheer my lone solitude with joyous gladness.*

The Macrology and Pleonasm

are as generally coupled as a lean rabbit with a fat one. Nor
is it a wonder the superfluity of words and the vacuity of
sense being just the same thing. I am pleased to see one of our
greatest adversaries employ this figure:

The growth of meadows, and the pride of fields.

The food of armies, and support of wars.

Refuse of swords, and gleanings of a fight.

Lessen his numbers, and contract his host.

Where'er his friends retire, or foes succeed.

Covered with tempests, and in oceans drowned.*

Of all which the perfection is:

The Tautology

Break thro' the billows, and – divide the main.*

In smoother numbers, and – in softer verse.*

Divide – and part – the severed world – in two.*

With ten thousand others equally musical, and plentifully flowing through most of our celebrated modern poems.

12

Of expression, and the several sorts
of style of the present age.

THE EXPRESSION IS ADEQUATE when it is proportionally
low to the profundity of the thought. It must not be
always grammatical, lest it appear pedantic and ungentle-
manly, nor too clear, for fear it become vulgar; for obscurity
bestows a cast of the wonderful and throws an oracular dig-
nity upon a piece which hath no meaning.

For example, sometimes use the wrong number: "The
sword and pestilence at once *devours*", instead of *devour*.
Sometimes the wrong case: "And who more fit to sooth the
god than *thee*", instead of *thou*. And rather than say, "Thetis
saw Achilles weep",* she *heard* him weep.

We must be exceeding careful in two things: first, in the
choice of low words; secondly, in the sober and orderly way
of ranging them. Many of our poets are naturally blessed
with this talent, insomuch that they are in the circumstance
of that honest citizen who had made prose all his life without

knowing it. Let verses run in this manner, just to be a vehicle to the words. I take them from my last cited author who, though otherwise by no means of our rank, seemed once in his life to have a mind to be simple.*

If not, a prize I will myself decree,
From him, or him, or else perhaps from thee.

...full of days was he:
Two ages past, he lived the third to see.

The king of forty kings, and honoured more
By mighty Jove than e'er was king before.

That I may know, if thou my prayer deny,
The most despised of all the gods am I.

Then let my mother once be ruled by me,
Tho' much more wise than I pretend to be.*

Or these of the same hand:

I leave the arts of poetry and verse
To them that practise them with more success:
Of greater truths I now prepare to tell,
And so at once, dear friend and muse, farewell.*

Sometimes a single word will familiarize a poetical idea – as where a ship set on fire owes all the spirit of the *bathos* to one choice word that ends the line:

> And his scorched ribs the hot contagion fried.*

And in that description of a world in ruins:

> Should the whole frame of nature round him break,
> He unconcerned would hear the mighty crack.*

So also in these:

> Beasts tame and savage to the river's brink
> Come from the fields and wild abodes – to drink.

Frequently two or three words will do it effectually:

> He from the clouds does the sweet liquor squeeze
> That cheers the forest and the garden trees.*

It is also useful to employ technical terms which estrange your style from the great and general ideas of nature. And the higher your subject is, the lower should you search into mechanics for your expression. If you describe the garment of an angel, say that his linen was "finely spun", and "bleached on the happy plains". Call an army of angels "angelic cuirassiers", and if you have occasion to mention a number of misfortunes, style them:

Fresh troops of pains and regimented woes.*

Style is divided by the rhetoricians into the proper and the figured. Of the figured we have already treated, and the proper is what our authors have nothing to do with. Of styles we shall mention only the principal, which owe to the moderns either their chief improvement or entire invention.

1. The Florid

Than which none is more proper to the *bathos*, as flowers – which are the lowest of vegetables – are the most gaudy and do many times grow in great plenty at the bottom of ponds and ditches.

A fine writer in this kind presents you with the following posy:

The groves appear all dressed with wreaths of flowers,
And from their leaves drop aromatic showers,

Whose fragrant heads in mystic twines above
Exchanged their sweets and mixed with thousand kisses,
As if the willing branches strove
To beautify and shade the grove.*

(Which indeed most branches do.) But this is still excelled by our Laureate.

Branches in branches twined compose the grove,
And shoot and spread, and blossom into love.
The trembling palms their mutual vows repeat,
And bending poplars bending poplars meet.
The distant platans seem to press more nigh
And, to the sighing alders, alders sigh.*

Hear also our Homer:

His robe of state is formed of light refined,
And endless train of lustre spreads behind.
His throne's of bright compacted glory made,
With pearl celestial, and with gems inlaid,
Whence floods of joy and seas of splendour flow,
On all th'angelic gazing throng below.*

2. The Pert Style

This does in as peculiar a manner become the low in wit as a pert air does the low in stature. Mr Thomas Brown, the author of the *London Spy*, and all the spies and trips in general, are herein to be diligently studied. In verse, Mr Cibber's *Prologues*.

But the beauty and energy of it is never so conspicuous as when it is employed in modernizing and adapting to the taste of the times the works of the ancients. This we rightfully phrase "doing them into English" and "making them English" – two expressions of great propriety, the one denoting our neglect of the manner how, the other the force and the compulsion with which it is brought about. It is by virtue of this style that Tacitus talks like a coffee-house politician, Josephus like the *British Gazetteer*, Tully is as short and smart as Seneca or Mr Asgill, Marcus Aurelius is excellent at snip-snap, and honest Thomas à Kempis as prim and polite as any preacher at court.

3. The À-la-Mode Style

Which is fine by being new, and has this happiness attending to it – that it is as durable and extensive as the poem itself. Take some examples of it, in the description of the sun in a mourning coach upon the death of Queen Mary:

> See Phoebus now, as once for Phaeton,
> Has masked his face, and put deep mourning on;
> Dark clouds his sable chariot do surround,
> And the dull steeds stalk o'er the melancholy round.*

Of Prince Arthur's soldiers drinking:

> While rich Burgundian wine and bright champagne,
> Chase from their minds the terrors of the main.

(Whence we also learn that Burgundy and champagne make a man on shore despise a storm at sea.)

Of the Almighty encamping his regiments:

> ...He sunk a vast capacious deep,
> Where he his liquid regiments does keep.
> Thither the waves file off, and make their way
> To form the mighty body of the sea;
> Where they encamp, and in their station stand
> Entrenched in works of rock and lines of sand.*

Of two armies on the point of engaging:

> Yon armies are the cards which both must play;
> At least come off a saver if you may:

Throw boldly at the sum the gods have set;
These on your side will all their fortunes bet.*

All perfectly agreeable to the present customs and best fashions of this our metropolis.

But the principal branch of the À-la-Mode is the Prurient, a style greatly advanced and honoured of late by the practice of persons of the first quality, and by the encouragement of the ladies not unsuccessfully introduced even into the drawing room. Indeed, its incredible progress and conquests may be compared to those of the great Sesostris, and are everywhere known by the same marks – the images of the genital parts of men or women. It consists wholly of metaphors drawn from two most fruitful sources or springs, the very *bathos* of the human body, that is to say *** and ****************** *hiatus magnus lachrymabilis.* ******************************** ******. And selling of bargains, and double entendre, and *Κιββερισμος,* and *Ολφιελδισμος,** all derived from the same sources.

4. The Finical

Which consists of the most curious, affected, mincing metaphors, and partakes of the last mentioned.

As this, of a brook dried by the sun:

Won by the summer's importuning ray,
Th'eloping stream did from her channel stray
And with enticing sunbeams stole away.

Of an easy death:

When watchful Death shall on his harvest look
And see thee ripe with age, invite the hook;
He'll gently cut thy bending stalk, and thee
Lay kindly in the grave, his granary.*

Of trees in a storm:

Oaks with extended arms the winds defy,
The tempest sees their strength and sighs, and passes by.*

Of water simmering over the fire:

The sparkling flames raise water to a smile,
Yet the pleased liquor pines, and lessens all the while.*

5.

Lastly, I shall place the Cumbrous, which moves heavily under
a load of metaphors and draws after it a long train of words.

And the Buskin, or Stately, frequently and with great felicity mixed with the former. For as the first is the proper engine to depress what is high, so is the second to raise what is base and low to a ridiculous visibility. When both these can be done at once, then is the *bathos* in perfection; as when a man is set with his head downwards and his breech upright his degradation is complete: one end of him is as high as ever, only that end is the wrong one. Will not every true lover of the profound be delighted to behold the most vulgar and low actions of life exalted in this manner?

Who knocks at the door?

> For whom thus rudely pleads my loud-tongued gate,
> That he may enter?...*

See who is there?

> Advance the fringèd curtains of thy eyes,
> And tell me who comes yonder...*

Shut the door.

> The wooden guardian of our privacy
> Quick on its axle turn...

CHAPTER 12

Bring my clothes.

> Bring me what Nature, tailor to the bear,
> To man himself denied: she gave me cold,
> But would not give me clothes...

Light the fire.

> Bring forth some remnant of Promethean theft,
> Quick to expand th'inclement air congealed
> By Boreas's rude breath...

Snuff the candle.

> Yon luminary amputation needs –
> Thus shall you save its half-extinguished life.*

Open the letter.

> Wax! Render up thy trust...*

Uncork the bottle and chip the bread.

> Apply thine engine to the spongy door,
> Set Bacchus from his glassy prison free,
> And strip white Ceres of her nut-brown coat.*

Appendix

13

A project for the advancement of the bathos.

T HUS HAVE I, my dear countrymen, with incredible pains and diligence, discovered the hidden sources of the *bathos* or, as I may say, broke open the abysses of this Great Deep. And having now established the good and wholesome laws, what remains but that all true moderns with their utmost might do proceed to put the same in execution? In order whereto, I think I shall in the second place highly deserve of my country, by proposing such a scheme as may facilitate this great end.

As our number is confessedly far superior to that of the enemy, there seems nothing wanting but unanimity among ourselves. It is therefore humbly offered that all and every individual of the *bathos* do enter into a firm association and incorporate into one regular body, whereof every member, even the meanest, will some way contribute to the support of the whole – in like manner as the weakest reeds, when joined in one bundle, become infrangible. To which end our art ought to be put upon the same foot with other arts of this age. The vast improvement of modern manufactures ariseth from their being divided into several branches, and parcelled out to several trades. For instance, in clockmaking, one artist makes the balance, another the spring, another the crown wheels, a fourth the case, and the principal workman puts all together. To this economy we owe the perfection of our modern watches, and doubtless we also might that of our modern poetry and rhetoric, were the several parts branched out in the like manner.

Nothing is more evident than that divers persons, no other way remarkable, have each a strong disposition to the formation of some particular trope or figure. Aristotle sayeth that the hyperbole is an ornament of speech fit for young men of quality – accordingly we find in those gentlemen a wonderful propensity towards it, which is marvellously improved by travelling. Soldiers also and seamen are very happy in the same figure. The periphrasis or circumlocution is the peculiar talent of country farmers, the proverb and apologue of old men at their clubs, the ellipsis – or speech by half-words – of ministers and politicians, the aposiopesis of courtiers, the litotes or diminution of ladies, whisperers and backbiters, and the anadiplosis of common criers and hawkers, who by redoubling the same words persuade people to buy their oysters, green hastings,* or new ballads. Epithets may be found in great plenty at Billingsgate, sarcasm and irony learnt upon the water, and the epiphenomena or exclamation frequently from the bear garden, and as frequently from the "Hear him" of the House of Commons.

Now each man applying his whole time and genius upon his particular figure would doubtless attain to perfection, and when each became incorporated and sworn into the society – as hath been proposed – a poet or orator would have no more to do but to send to the particular traders in each kind: to the metaphorist for his allegories, to the simile-maker for his comparisons, to the ironist for his sarcasms, to the apophthegmatist for his sentences, etc., whereby a dedication or speech would be composed in a moment, the superior artist having nothing to do but put together all the materials.

I therefore propose that there be contrived with all convenient dispatch, at the public expense, a rhetorical chest of drawers consisting of three storeys: the highest for the deliberative, the middle for the demonstrative and the lowest for the judicial. These shall be divided into loci or places, being repositories for matter and argument in the several kinds of oration or writing, and every drawer shall again be subdivided into cells resembling those of cabinets for rarities. The apartment for peace or war, and that of the liberty of the press, may in a very few days be filled with several arguments perfectly new, and the vituperative partition will as easily be replenished with a most choice collection, entirely of the growth and manufacture of the present age. Every composer will soon be taught the use of this cabinet and how to manage all the registers of it, which will be drawn out much in the manner of those of an organ.

The keys of it must be kept in honest hands, by some reverend prelate or valiant officer of unquestioned loyalty and affection to every present establishment in Church and State, which will sufficiently guard against any mischief which might otherwise be apprehended from it.

And being lodged in such hands, it may be at discretion let out by the day to several great orators in both houses, from whence it is to be hoped much profit or gain will also accrue to our society.

14

How to make dedications, panegyrics or satires,
and of the colours of honourable and dishonourable.

NOW OF WHAT NECESSITY the foregoing project may prove will appear from this single consideration: that nothing is of equal consequence to the success of our works as speed and dispatch. Great pity it is that solid brains are not, like other solid bodies, constantly endowed with a velocity in sinking proportioned to their heaviness. For it is with the flowers of the *bathos* as with those of Nature – which, if the careful gardener brings not hastily to the market in the morning, must unprofitably perish and wither before night. And of all our productions none is so short-lived as the dedication and panegyric, which are often but the praise of a day, and become by the next utterly useless, improper, indecent and false. This is the more to be lamented, inasmuch as they are the very two sorts whereon in a manner depends that gain or profit which must still be remembered to be the whole end of our writers and speakers.

We shall therefore employ this chapter in showing the quickest method of composing them; after which we will teach a short way to epic poetry. And these being confessedly the works of most importance and difficulty, it is presumed we may leave the rest to each author's own learning or practice.

First of panegyric. Every man is honourable who is so by law, custom or title: the public are better judges of what is honourable than private men. The virtues of great men, like those of plants, are inherent in them whether they are exerted or not, and the more strongly inherent the less they are exerted, as man is the more rich the less he spends.

All great ministers, without either private or economical virtue, are virtuous by their posts, liberal and generous upon the public money, provident upon parliamentary supplies, just by paying public interest, courageous and magnanimous by the fleets and armies, magnificent upon the public expenses and prudent by public success. They have by their office a right to a share of the public stock of virtues; besides, they are by prescription immemorial invested in all the celebrated virtues of their predecessors in the same stations, especially those of their own ancestors.

As to what are commonly called the colours of honourable and dishonourable, they are various in different countries – in this they are blue, green and red. But forasmuch as the duty we owe to the public doth often require that we should put some things in a strong light and throw a shade over others, I shall explain the method of turning a vicious man into a hero.

The first and chief rule is the golden rule of transformation, which consists in converting vices into their bordering virtues. A man who is a spendthrift and will not pay a just debt may have his injustice transformed into liberality, cowardice may be metamorphose into prudence, intemperance into good nature and good fellowship, corruption into patriotism, and lewdness into tenderness and facility.

The second is the rule of contraries. It is certain the less a man is endued with any virtue, the more need he has to have it plentifully bestowed, especially those good qualities of which the world generally believes he hath none at all – for who will thank a man for giving him what he *has*?

The reverse of these precepts will serve for satire, wherein we are ever to remark that whoso loseth his place or becomes out of favour with the government, hath forfeited his share of public praise and honour. Therefore, the truly public-spirited writer ought in duty to strip him whom the government has stripped, which is the real poetical justice of this age. For a full collection of topics and epithets to be used in the praise and dispraise of ministerial and unministerial persons, I refer to our rhetorical cabinet, concluding with an earnest exhortation to all my brethren to observe the precepts here laid down – the neglect of which hath cost some of them their ears in a pillory.

15

A receipt to make an epic poem.

AN EPIC POEM, the critics agree, is the greatest work human nature is capable of. They have already laid down many mechanical rules for compositions of this sort, but at the same time they cut off almost all undertakers from the possibility of ever performing them, for the first qualification they unanimously require in a poet is a genius. I shall here endeavour, for the benefit of my countrymen, to make it manifest that epic poems may be made without a genius – nay, without learning or much reading. This must necessarily be of great use to all those who confess they never read, and of whom the world is convinced they never learn. What Molière observes of making a dinner – that any man can do it with money, and if a professed cook cannot do it *without* he has his art for nothing* – the same may be said of making a poem: 'tis easily brought about by him that has a genius, but the skill lies in doing it without one. In pursuance of this end, I shall present the reader with a plain and certain recipe, by which any author in the *bathos* may be qualified for this grand performance.

For the Fable

Take out of any old poem, history book, romance or legend (for instance *Geoffrey of Monmouth* or *Don Belianis of Greece*) those parts of story which afford most scope for long descriptions. Put these pieces together, and throw all the adventures you fancy into one tale. Then take a hero, whom you may choose for the sound of his name, and put him into the midst of these adventures. There let him work for twelve books, at the end of which you may take him out, ready-prepared to conquer or to marry, it being necessary that the conclusion of an epic poem be fortunate.

To Make an Episode

Take any remaining adventure of your former collection, in which you could in no way involve your hero, or any unfortunate accident that was too good to be thrown away, and it will be of use, applied to any other person, who may be lost and evaporate in the course of the work without the least damage to the composition.

For the Moral and Allegory

These you may extract out of the fable afterwards, at your leisure. Be sure you strain them sufficiently.

For the Manners

For those of the hero, take all the best qualities you can find in the most celebrated heroes of antiquity: if they will not be reduced to a consistency, lay them all on a heap upon him. But be sure that they are qualities which your patron would be thought to have, and to prevent any mistake which the world may be subject to, select from the alphabet those capital letters that compose his name, and set them at the head of a dedication before your poem. However, do not absolutely observe the exact quantity of these virtues, it not being determined whether or no it be necessary for the hero of a poem to be an honest man. For the under-characters, gather them from Homer and Virgil, and change the names as occasion serves.

For the Machines

Take of deities, male and female, as many as you can use. Separate them into two equal parts and keep Jupiter in the middle. Let Juno put him in a ferment and Venus mollify him. Remember on all occasions to make use of volatile Mercury. If you have need of devils, draw them out of Milton's Paradise, and extract your spirits from Tasso. The use of these machines is evident, for since no epic poem can possibly subsist without them, the wisest way is to reserve them for your greatest necessities. When you cannot extricate your hero by any human means, or yourself by your own wit, seek relief from Heaven, and the gods will do your business very readily. This is according to the direct prescription of Horace in his *Art of Poetry*.

*Nec Deus intersit, nisi dignus vindice nodus inciderit.**

That is to say, "A poet should never call upon the gods for their assistance but when he is in great perplexity".

For the Descriptions

For a tempest. Take Eurus, Zephyr, Auster and Boreas, and cast them together in one verse. Add to these of rain, lightning and of thunder (the loudest you can) *quantum sufficit*. Mix your clouds and billows well together till they foam, and thicken your description here and there with a quicksand. Brew your tempest well in your head, before you set it a-blowing.

For a battle. Pick a large quantity of images and descriptions from Homer's *Iliad*, with a spice or two of Virgil, and if there remain any overplus, you may lay them by for a skirmish. Season it well with similes, and it will make an excellent battle.

For a burning town. If such a description be necessary – because it is certain there is one in Virgil – old Troy is ready-burnt to your hands. But if you fear that would be thought borrowed, a chapter or two of the *Theory of the Conflagration*, well circumstanced and done into verse, will be a good *succedaneum*.

As for similes and metaphors, they may be found all over the creation. The most ignorant may gather them, but the danger is in applying them. For this advise with your bookseller.

16

A project for the advancement of the stage.

I T MAY BE THOUGHT that we should not wholly omit the drama, which makes so great and so lucrative a part of poetry. But this province is so well taken care of by the present managers of the theatre that it is perfectly needless to suggest to them any other methods than they have already practised for the advancement of the *bathos*.

Here, therefore, in the name of all our brethren, let me return our most sincere and humble thanks to the most august Mr B***t***n B***th, the most serene Mr W***ll***m W***lks, and the most undaunted Mr C***ll***y C***bb***r – of whom let it be known when the people of this age shall be ancestors, and to all the succession of our successors, that to this present day they continue to outdo even their own outdoings. And when the inevitable hand of sweeping Time shall have brushed off all the works of today, may this testimony of a contemporary critic to their fame be extended as far as tomorrow!

Yet, if to so wise an administration it be possible anything can be added, it is that more ample and comprehensive scheme which Mr D***nn***s and Mr Gildon (the two greatest critics and reformers then living) made public in the year 1720, in a project signed with their names and dated the 2nd of February. I cannot better conclude than by presenting the reader with the substance of it.

1. It is proposed that the two theatres be incorporated into one company; that the Royal Academy of Music be added to them as an orchestra; and that Mr Figg with his prize-fighters and Violante with the rope-dancers be admitted in partnership.

2. That a spacious building be erected at the public expense, capable of containing at least ten thousand spectators, which is become absolutely necessary by the great addition of children and nurses to the audience since the new entertainments. That there be a stage as large as the Athenian, which was near ninety thousand geometrical paces square, and separate divisions for the two Houses of Parliament, my lords the judges, the honourable the Directors of the Academy, and the Court of Aldermen, who shall have their places frank.

3. If Westminster Hall be not allotted to this service – which, by reason of its proximity to the two chambers

of Parliament above mentioned, seems not altogether improper – it is left to the wisdom of the nation whether Somerset House may not be demolished and a theatre built upon that site, which lies convenient to receive spectators from the county of Surrey, who may be wafted thither by water carriage, esteemed by all projectors the cheapest whatsoever. To this may be added that the river Thames may in the readiest manner convey those eminent personages from courts beyond the seas who may be drawn either by curiosity to behold some of our most celebrated pieces, or by affection to see their countrymen the harlequins and eunuchs, of which convenient notice may be given for two or three months before in the public prints.

4. That the theatre abovesaid be environed with a fair quadrangle of buildings, fitted for the accommodation of decayed critics and poets, out of whom six of the most aged – their age to be computed from the year wherein their first work was published – shall be elected to manage the affairs of the society, provided nevertheless that the Laureate for the time being may be always one. The head or president over all – to prevent disputes, but too frequent among the learned – shall be the oldest poet and critic to be found in the whole island.

5. The male players are to be lodged in the garrets of the said quadrangle and to attend the persons of the poets

dwelling under them by brushing their apparel, drawing on their shoes and the like. The actresses are to make their beds and wash their linen.

6. A large room shall be set apart for a library, to consist of all the modern dramatic poems, and all the criticisms extant. In the midst of this room shall be a round table for the Council of Six to sit and deliberate on the merits of plays. The majority shall determine the dispute, and if it should happen that three and three should be of each side, the president shall have a casting voice, unless where the contention may run so high as to require a decision by single combat.

7. It may be convenient to place the Council of Six in some conspicuous situation in the theatre, where after the manner usually practised by composers in music, they may give signs – before settled and agreed upon – of dislike or approbation. In consequence of these signs the whole audience shall be required to clap or hiss, that the town may learn certainly when and how far they ought to be pleased.

8. It is submitted whether it would not be proper to distinguish the Council of Six by some particular habit or gown of an honourable shape and colour, to which might be added a square cap and a white wand.

9. That to prevent unmarried actresses making away with their infants, a competent provision be allowed for the

nurture of them, who shall for that reason be deemed the "Children of the Society", and that they may be educated according to the genius of their parents, the said actresses shall declare upon oath – as far as their memory will allow – the true names and qualities of their several fathers. A private gentleman's son shall at the public expense be brought up a page to attend the Council of Six. A more ample provision shall be made for the son of a poet, and a greater still for the son of a critic.

10. If it be discovered that any actress is got with child during the interludes of any play wherein she hath a part, it shall be reckoned a neglect of her business, and she shall forfeit accordingly. If any actor for the future shall commit murder, except upon the stage, he shall be left to the laws of the land – the like is to be understood of robbery and theft. In all other cases, particularly in those of debt, it is proposed that this, like the other courts of Whitehall and St James's, may be held a "place of privilege", and whereas it has been found that an obligation to satisfy paltry creditors has been a discouragement to men of letters, if any person of quality or others shall send for any poet or critic of this society to any remote quarter of the town, the said poet or critic shall freely pass and repass without being liable to an arrest.

11. The aforementioned scheme in its several regulations may be supported by profits arising from every third night

throughout the year. And as it would be hard to suppose that so many persons could live without any food – though from the former course of their lives a very little will be sufficient – the masters of calculation will, we believe, agree that out of those profits the said persons might be subsisted in a sober and decent manner. We will venture to affirm further that not only the proper magazines of thunder and lightning, but paint, diet drinks, spitting pots and all other necessaries of life may in like manner fairly be provided for.

12. If some of the articles may at first view seem liable to objections, particularly those that give so vast a power to the Council of Six – which is indeed larger than any entrusted to the great officers of state – this may be obviated by swearing those six persons of His Majesty's Privy Council and obliging them to pass everything of moment previously at that most honourable board.

Vale & Fruere,

MAR. SCRIB.

Note on the Text

The text in the present edition of *Peri Bathous* has been reproduced from the first edition of the Swift-Pope *Miscellanies*, 'The Last Volume', published by Motte in 1727/8. This edition appears to have been hastily put together and carelessly printed. We have silently corrected many typographical errors and updated the spelling whenever appropriate to avoid ambiguity. We are greatly indebted to the 1952 Columbia University Press facsimile edition of the work, annotated by Edna Leake Steeves, from which many of our own notes have drawn useful information.

Notes

p. 3, *my dear countrymen*: Martinus Scriblerus, though of German extraction, was born in England. *Vid.* his *Life and Memoirs*, which will speedily be published. (ALEXANDER POPE'S NOTE).

p. 3, ...*their ὕψος*: The first of many references to and deliberate misquotations of the work of Longinus – the name given to the unknown author of *On the Sublime*, or *Perì hýpsos*, a treatise on aesthetics written between the first and third centuries AD. Pope's *Peri Bathous* is a parody of this classical text.

p. 5, *master of Alexander... Zenobia*: Aristotle (384 BC–322 BC) and Longinus (*fl.* first century).

p. 6, *toto cœlo*: "Diametrically" (Latin).

p. 8, *Et prodesse... Pœtae*: Horace (65–68 BC), *Ars Poetica*, l. 333.

p. 9, *Nascimur poetæ*: "We are born poets" (Latin). The quotation, which is from Horace, continues "*fimus oratores*" ("by education we become orators").

p. 10, *maxim... Horace*: "*Mediocribus esse poetis / Non di, non homines etc.*" – "Not gods, nor men, nor even booksellers have tolerated second-rate poets" (Latin). *Ars Poetica*, ll. 372–73. (ALEXANDER POPE'S NOTE)

p. 10, *...alacrity of sinking*: Falstaff: "You may know by my size that I have a kind of alacrity in sinking." William Shakespeare, *Merry Wives of Windsor*, Act III, Sc. 5, ll. 13–14.

p. 13, *goût de travers*: "Skewed taste" (French). Phoebe Clinket: "Ah, what a *goût de travers* rules the understandings of the illiterate!" John Gay, *Three Hours after Marriage*.

p. 14, *Serpentes avibus... agni*: "Serpents should be coupled with birds, or lambs with tigers" (Latin). *Ars Poetica*, ll. 120–21

p. 14, *harlequins and magicians on our stage*: An allusion to the competing pantomimes of John Rich (1682–1761) and Colley Cibber (1671–1757), the latter an actor and playwright who went on to become Poet Laureate in 1730.

p. 16, *The skies... The ocean joyed... Glorious illuminations... flung*: Sir Richard Blackmore, *Prince Arthur* (Fourth Edition Revised, London 1714), pp. 41–42; p. 14; p. 50.

p. 16, *Look down... we stray*: Ambrose Philips, 'Lament for Queen Mary'.

p. 17, *Thus have I seen... fun'ral nest*: Not identified. It has been suggested that these, and other untraced passages within this work, are quotations from Pope's own early poetry, particularly his epic poem, *Alcander*.

p. 19, *Sometimes the Lord... Th'almighty Chemist... bread*: Sir Richard Blackmore, *A Paraphrase on the Book of Job: as Likewise on the Songs of Moses, Deborah, David, on Six Select Psalms, Some Chapters of Isaiah, and the Third Chapter of Habakkuk*, (Second Edition Revised, London, 1716), hereafter *Job*, p. 172; p. 263; p. 75; p. 170; p. 70; p. 61; p. 298: "God will not be" should read "He'll be no more"; p. 181; p. 180; p. 174; p. 131; p. 218.

p. 22, *authors to compare them*: Pope only gave these authors' initials, and never identified them by name. Still, attempts to put names to the initials have been made, and the suggestions are included in the following notes.

p. 22, *flying fishes... G.S., A.H., C.G.*: G.S. – George Stepney (1663–1707), George Sewell (1673–1726) or the Reverend

Dr George Stanhope (1660–1728). A.H. – Anthony Hammond (1668–1738) or Aaron Hill (1683–1750). C.G. – Charles Gildon (1665–1724).

p. 22, *swallows... L.T., W.P., Lord R.*: L.T. – Lewis Theobald (1688–1704). W.P. – William Pattison (1706–27), William Philips (d. 1724) or William Pulteney (1684–1764). Lord R. – John Wilmot, Earl of Rochester (1647–80), Wentworth Dillon, Earl of Roscommon (1633–85).

p. 23, *ostriches... D.F., L.E., the Hon. E.H.*: D.F. – Daniel Defoe (*c*.1659–1731). L.E. – Lawrence Eusden (1688–1730). The Hon E.H. – the Hon. Edward Howard, 8th Earl of Suffolk (d. 1732).

p. 23, *parrots... W.B., W.H., C.C., the Reverend D.D.*: W.B. – William Broome (1689–1745). W.H. – William Harrison (1685–1713) or the Revd Walter Harte (1709–74). C.C. – Colley Cibber (1671–1757). The Reverend D.D. – The Revd Dean Daniel (1681–1739).

p. 23, *didappers... L.W. — D. Esq., the Hon. Sir W.Y.*: Sources disagree as to whether "L.W. — D. Esq." comprises only one set of initials, or two. Either way, it has been suggested they could stand for Leonard Welsted (1688–1747). If "— D. Esq." is to be read separately it could stand for George Duckett (1684–1732) or George Bubb Doddington, Baron Melcombe (1691–1762). The Hon. Sir W.Y. – Sir William Yonge (d. 1755).

p. 23, *porpoises… J.D., C.G., J.O.*: J.D. – John Dennis (1657–1734). C.G. – Charles Gildon. J.O. – John Oldmixon (1673–1742).

p. 23, *frogs… E.W., J.M. Esq., T.D. Gent.*: E.W. – Edward Ward (1667–1731). J.M. Esq. – James Moore-Smythe (1702–34); or Charles Johnson (1679–1748) and Joseph Mitchell (1684–1738). T.D. Gent. – Tom Durfey (1652–1723).

p. 23, *eels… L.W., L.T., P.M., General C.*: L.W. and L.T. – Leonard Welsted and Lewis Theobald. P.M. – Peter Anthony Motteux (1660–1718). General C. – Christopher Codrington (1668–1710).

p. 23, *tortoises… A.P., W.B., L.E., the Rt. Hon. E. of S.*: A.P. – Ambrose Philips (1674–1749). The Rt. Hon. E. of S. – Charles Douglas, 2nd Earl of Selkirk (1663–1739).

p. 25, *Mr Curll*: Edmund Curll (1675–1747), an infamous bookseller of Pope's day, who specialized in pornographic pamphlets and libellous biographies.

p. 26, *triticalness*: "Tritical" was a play upon the words "trite" and "critical", c.f. *A Tritical Essay upon the Faculties of the Mind* in Jonathan Swift's *Miscellanies* of 1711.

p. 27, *She drinks… Venus beheld her… Hears his own feet… fore*: Not traced. The lines beginning "Venus beheld her" may have originally stood in Pope's *Windsor Forest*. It is also possible that Pope simply invented all of these lines for the purpose of illustrating his points within this work.

p. 27, *None but himself… parallel*: Lewis Theobald, *Double Falsehood*, Act II, Sc. 1.

p. 28, *So fair thou art… Thus Phoebus… day*: William Broome 'On the Birthday of Mr Robert Trefusis' (1712); 'Epistle to my Friend Mr Elijah Fenton' (1726).

p. 30, *With teats distended… In flaming heaps… blue*: *Job*, p. 133; *Prince Arthur*, p. 89.

p. 30, *His eyeballs burn… deck his mane*: Possibly another invention of Pope's, or perhaps lines taken from a contemporary author's paraphrase of *Job*; either way, Blackmore did not write these lines.

p. 31, *They brandish high… A waving sea… fed*: *Prince Arthur*, p. 197; *Job*, p. 78.

p. 31, *Nature's confectioner… garden into gold*: John Cleveland, 'Fuscara'.

p. 32, *Little siren… vocal spell*: Ambrose Philips, 'To Signora Cuzzonio'.

p. 33, *Canst thou set… The hills… behind*: *Job*, p. 180; Psalm 104, p. 267.

p. 35, *De F***…E***n of Bl***k***re*: De F*** – Daniel Defoe. Withers – George Withers (1588–1667). T***te – Nahum Tate (1652–1715). Ogilby – John Ogilby (1600–76). E. W***rd – Edward Ward. John Taylor (1580–1653). E***n – Lawrence Eusden. Bl***k***re – Sir Richard Blackmore.

p. 35, *A. Ph***... Mr W***st***d*: A. Ph*** – Ambrose Philips. Mr W***st***d – Leonard Welsted.

p. 36, *Horrificis juxta tonat... exaestuat imo*: *Aeneid*, III, 571–77.

p. 37, *Etna, and all the... spread the ground*: *Prince Arthur*, p. 75.

p. 37, Horace... *stars*: *Sublimi feriam sidera vertice* – "I strike the stars with my sublime head" (Latin). Horace, *Carmina*, I, 1, 36. (ALEXANDER POPE'S NOTE)

p. 37, *Empedocles... Etna*: The death of Empedocles, according to legend caused by him throwing himself into the active volcano of Mount Etna, is referred to by Horace in his *Ars Poetica* as an example of the madness of poets.

p. 37, *And so... Master Lieutenant*: Nicholas Rowe, *Lady Jane Grey*, Act v, Sc. 1, l. 36.

p. 43, *cosins... bubble boy... tompion... colmar... toupee*: Stays, tweezer case, watch, fan and a sort of periwig: all words in use this present year 1727. (ALEXANDER POPE'S NOTE) The source of the quotation has not been traced.

p. 43, *a T***m-T***dman... a whitestaff*: A Tom-Turdman, a slang term for one whose job was to empty "necessary houses" or toilets. Whitestaff was a term for certain high-ranking public officials who carried a white staff as a badge of office.

p. 44, *The lords... talk big*: Nathaniel Lee (1653–92), *The Rival Queens; or, Alexander the Great*, Act i, Sc. 1.

p. 47, *Tho' he... The stones and all... waste*: *Job*, pp. 91 and 93: "Soon shall he perish" should read "Th'unrighteous perish"; p. 22; pp. 289 and 291–92; *Prince Arthur*, p. 73; *Job*, p. 107; *Prince Arthur*, p. 157: "Upon the shore" should read "Along the coast"; *Job*, p. 89.

p. 47, *While the kind... to 'scape*: Edmund Waller, *Poems*, 11th edn. (1727) p. 93.

p. 48, *Sadly they charm... they please*: Richard Steele, *The Procession. A Poem on Her Majesty's Funeral*.

p. 48, *His eyes... the light*: Francis Quarles, 'On the Body of Man', in *Divine Fancies*, i, 42.

p. 48, *The gods... so red*: Nathaniel Lee, *Sophonisba*, Act i; "The gods look" should read "And then looked".

p. 48, *The fairies... o'er the green*: Ambrose Philips, 'Sixth Pastoral', in *Poetical Miscellanies* (1709).

p. 48, *All nature... mountains rock*: *Job*, p. 176.

p. 50, *He roared so loud... The silver whiteness... black*: Not traced.

p. 50, *Th'obscureness... all one light*: Lewis Theobald, *Double Falsehood*, Act i, Sc. 3.

p. 50, *Up to the stars... the frighted sky*: *Prince Arthur* (1695), p. 232.

p. 51, *Behold... Ye Gods!... I'd call... high*: Not traced.

p. 52, *Under the tropics... received our yoke*: Edmund Waller, *Poems*, p. 119.

p. 52, *And thou... Earl of Mar*: Has been attributed to Pope's *Alcander*, but the untraced source is probably Scottish, as are the Earldoms of Dalhousie and Mar.

p. 52, *Nor death... fortified redoubt*: Misquotation of John Dennis's 'A Pindarick Ode on the King', *Miscellanies in Verse and Prose* (1693), p. 13. The original read: *Nor Art nor Nature has the force / To stop its noisy course / Nor Alps, nor Pyreneans keep it out / Nor fortified redoubt.*

p. 54, *His motion works... Now the resisted flames... The mighty stuffa... I cannot stifle... Distended with the waters... unrent*: *Job*, p. 197; *Prince Arthur*, pp. 156–157; *King Arthur*, 1st edn. (1697), p. 103; *Job*, p. 41; *Job*, 1st edn. (1700) – the last line originally read: *Their wombs hang low in air, but are not rent.*

p. 55, *Little charm... of happy men, etc.*: The first six lines are from Ambrose Philips, 'To Miss Georgiana, Youngest Daughter to Lord Carteret'; the next ten are from 'To the Honourable Miss Carteret'.

p. 56, *Teach me to grieve... That ever she could die... I love in secret... Ye brighter maids... Ah silly I... To the grave senate... He whom loud cannon... majesty*: Ambrose Philips, 'Fourth Pastoral', ll. 49–51; 'Fourth Pastoral', ll. 49–51; 'Sixth Pastoral', ll. 45–47; 'Fourth Pastoral', ll. 63–66: "death" should read "hour"; 'Second Pastoral', ll. 61–62; 'Lament for Queen Mary'. The original read: *He whom the terrours of a bloody fight... / Nor the loud cannon's roar can terrifie/ falls from the grandeur of his majesty.*

p. 57, *The noise returning... dispelled the night*: Not traced.

p. 57, *The glories of... by break of day*: Possibly from one of Colley Cibber's plays, but remains as yet untraced.

p. 57, *Th'umbrageous shadow... joyous gladness*: Not traced. Probably written by Pope himself.

p. 58, *The growth of meadows... The food of armies... Refuse of swords... Lessen his numbers... Where'er his friends... Covered with tempests... drowned*: Joseph Addison, *Campaign* (1704) ll. 168; 190; 192; 199; 202; 268.

p. 58, *Break... divide the main*: Thomas Tickell, 'The Royal Progress'.

p. 58, *In smoother numbers... softer verse*: Joseph Addison, 'An Account of the Great English Poets. To Mr H.S. April 3, 1694'.

p. 58, *Divide... in two*: Anonymous, 'Horace, Ode III, Book III'. Later attributed to Addison.

p. 59, *The sword... And who more fit... Thetis saw Achilles weep*: *Iliad*, I, ll. 80, 178, 407, in *The First Book of Homer's Iliad*, "Translated by Mr Tickell" (1715).

p. 60, *I take them... to be simple*: Possibly an apology to Addison, rather than Tickell.

p. 60, *If not, a prize... ...full of days was he... The king of forty kings... That I may know... Then let my mother... be*: Tickell's *Iliad*, I, ll. 167–68; 292–93; 322–23; 594–95; 666–67.

p. 60, *I leave the arts... muse, farewell*: Addison, 'An Account of the Greatest English Poets'.

p. 61, *And his scorched ribs... contagion fried*: Prince Arthur, p. 151.

p. 61, *Should the whole... mighty crack*: Addison's 'Horace, Ode III, Book III'.

p. 61, *Beasts tame and savage... He from the clouds... trees*: Psalm 104, *Job*, p. 262; p. 264.

p. 62, *finely spun... bleached... angelic cuirassiers... Fresh troops... woes*: Prince Arthur, p. 19; p. 239; *Job*, p. 286. "Fresh" should read "Fierce".

p. 63, *The groves appear... shade the grove*: Apra Behn, 'The Golden Age', *Poems upon Several Occasions* (1684).

p. 63, *Branches in branches... alders sigh*: Lawrence Eusden's translation of Claudian's 'Court of Venus' (1713).

p. 63, *His robe of state... throng below*: Psalm 104, in *Job*, p. 260.

p. 65, *See Phoebus now... melancholy round*: 'Lament for Queen Mary', ll. 66–69.

p. 65, *While rich Burgundian... He sunk a vast... sand*: Prince Arthur, p. 16; Psalm 104, *Job*, pp. 261–62.

p. 66, *Yon armies... fortunes bet*: First two lines, *Sophonisba*, Act ɪv, Sc. 1. Last two lines, *Sophonisba*, Act ɪɪ, Sc. 2.

p. 66, *Κιββερισμος... Ολφιελδισμος*: Cibberism and Old-fieldism. Referring to Colley Cibber and Anne Oldfield (1683–1730).

p. 67, *Won by the summer's... When watchful death... granary*: *Job*, p. 26. "Stream" should read "flood", and "her", "its"; p. 23.

p. 67, *Oaks with extended... and passes by*: Dennis, 'Upon our Victory at Sea': "Oaks with extended" should read "Their huge extended".

p. 67, *The sparkling flames... all the while*: Anonymous, 'The Celebrated Beauties'.

p. 68, *For whom thus... may enter*: Not traced.

p. 68, *Advance the fringèd... comes yonder*: Dryden-Davenant's version of Shakespeare's *Tempest* (Scott-Saintsbury edn. of Dryden's *Works*, ɪɪɪ, 169): *Advance the fringed curtains of thine eyes / And say what thou seest yonder.*

p. 69, *The wooden guardian... Bring me what Nature... Bring forth... Yon luminary... life*: Not traced.

p. 69, *Wax! Render up thy trust*: Theobald, *Double Falsehood*, Act ɪɪ, Sc. 2.

p. 69, *Apply thine engine... nut-brown coat*: Not traced.

p. 74, *green hastings*: Early fruits and vegetables, specifically a kind of early green peas.

p. 81, *What Molière observes… art for nothing*: *L'Avare*, Act III, Sc. 1.

p. 84, *Nec Deus… nodus inciderit*: *Ars Poetica*, ll. 191–92.